NVIDIA'S CHAT QA 270B
Everything You Need to Know

An In-Depth Look at the New AI Powerhouse and What It Means for the Future

Alejandro S. Diego

Copyright © Alejandro S. Diego, 2024.

All rights reserved. No part of this publication may be reproduced, distributed, or transmitted in any form or by any means, including photocopying, recording, or other electronic or mechanical methods, without the prior written permission of the publisher, except in the case of brief quotations embodied in critical reviews and certain other noncommercial uses permitted by copyright law.

Table of Contents

Introduction   4
Chapter 1: Understanding Llama 3 Chat QA 270B   7
Chapter 2: Technical Specifications and Capabilities   11
Chapter 3: The Power of Retrieval-Augmented Generation (RAG)   21
Chapter 4: Diverse Applications of Llama 3 Chat QA 270B   30
Chapter 5: Performance Highlights and Limitations   35
Chapter 6: Environmental and Ethical Considerations   40
Chapter 7: Future Prospects and Societal Impact   45
Chapter 8: Navigating Ethical AI Development   51
Chapter 9: Collaborative AI Systems   57
Chapter 10: Privacy and Data Security   63
Chapter 11: The Road Ahead   69
Conclusion   76

Introduction

In a world where technology evolves at breakneck speed, standing at the forefront of innovation is both exhilarating and challenging. Imagine a tool so powerful that it can revolutionize the way we interact with information, transforming industries, and reshaping our daily lives. Welcome to the future, powered by Nvidia's Chat QA 270B.

As we embark on this journey, let's pause and marvel at the marvels of modern artificial intelligence. AI is no longer a distant dream; it is here, intricately woven into the fabric of our existence. Nvidia's Chat QA 270B is not just another AI model; it represents a quantum leap in understanding and processing complex information, promising to redefine our expectations of what AI can achieve.

Picture a world where long-form content creation is as effortless as a conversation with a friend, where legal professionals can sift through entire libraries in seconds, and where personalized learning is tailored to each individual's needs and pace. The advent of Nvidia's Chat QA 270B heralds this new era. Its capabilities extend beyond mere computational power; it possesses an unprecedented ability to handle long contexts, making it an indispensable ally in tasks that require deep understanding and nuanced responses.

The importance of AI in today's world cannot be overstated. From healthcare to finance, education to customer service, AI's transformative potential is boundless. Nvidia's Chat QA 270B stands as a testament to this potential, embodying years of research, innovation, and dedication. This model is poised to become a cornerstone in the AI landscape, offering solutions that were once the realm of science fiction.

This book is your guide to understanding the intricacies and possibilities of Nvidia's Chat QA 270B. We will explore its development, delve into its technical prowess, and uncover the myriad applications that make it a game-changer. Along the way, we will address the ethical considerations and future prospects that accompany such powerful technology. Our journey will be comprehensive, insightful, and, most importantly, engaging.

Prepare yourself for a thrilling exploration of AI's cutting edge. Whether you are a tech enthusiast, a professional seeking to harness AI's potential, or simply curious about the future, this book promises to enlighten and inspire. As we turn each page, the story of Nvidia's Chat QA 270B will unfold, revealing a world where technology enhances human capabilities and drives unprecedented progress.

Welcome to the future. Welcome to Nvidia's Chat QA 270B. Let the journey begin.

Chapter 1: Understanding Llama 3 Chat QA 270B

Nvidia's Chat QA 270B stands as a beacon of innovation in the rapidly evolving landscape of artificial intelligence. This groundbreaking model, developed by Nvidia's team of visionary researchers, is built upon Meta's Llama 3 framework, representing a significant leap in AI capabilities. The journey of its development is a testament to human ingenuity and the relentless pursuit of technological excellence.

The story of Llama 3 Chat QA 270B begins with the vision to create an AI model that surpasses the existing limitations of long-context understanding and retrieval-augmented generation. Nvidia's researchers embarked on a mission to push the boundaries, leveraging the robust foundation provided by Meta's Llama 3 framework. This framework, renowned for its ability to handle complex tasks, served as the perfect canvas for Nvidia's innovations.

One of the most remarkable features of Llama 3 Chat QA 270B is its impressive token capacity. With the ability to process 128,000 tokens, this model can handle approximately 100 pages of text seamlessly. This capacity is not just a numerical achievement; it signifies the model's prowess in managing and understanding extensive information without losing coherence. This capability is a game-changer, enabling the model to tackle tasks that were previously considered too complex for AI.

But the brilliance of Llama 3 Chat QA 270B extends beyond its raw power. It excels in versatility, adeptly managing long-form tasks while also adapting to medium-length and short-context scenarios. Whether it's a 32,000-token medium-length task or a concise 4,000-token query, this model handles each with equal finesse. This versatility ensures its applicability across a wide range of AI applications, making it a valuable tool for diverse industries and use cases.

The development of Llama 3 Chat QA 270B involved a meticulous process aimed at enhancing its long-context processing capabilities. Nvidia's team employed a two-step approach, starting with pre-training the model on a mix of data that emphasized long sequences. This foundational step laid the groundwork for the model's extended context abilities. The second phase involved a three-stage instruction tuning process, which honed the model's ability to apply its vast knowledge creatively and effectively to real-world tasks.

This structured approach to development resulted in a model that is not only powerful but also highly efficient in its application. The integration of retrieval-augmented generation (RAG) further elevates its capabilities, allowing it to break down large tasks into manageable chunks and retrieve relevant information as needed. This approach mimics human problem-solving, making Llama 3 Chat QA 270B a formidable tool in scenarios requiring deep, contextual understanding.

In essence, Llama 3 Chat QA 270B is a culmination of cutting-edge research, innovative techniques, and a vision for the future of AI. Its ability to handle extensive information, coupled with its versatility and efficiency, positions it as a revolutionary model in the AI domain. As we continue to explore its features and applications, the true impact of this technological marvel becomes increasingly evident, promising to reshape industries and redefine possibilities.

Chapter 2: Technical Specifications and Capabilities

The technical specifications of Nvidia's Chat QA 270B are nothing short of impressive, showcasing a blend of advanced technology and meticulous engineering. This AI model, developed on the Meta Llama 3 framework, is designed to push the boundaries of what artificial intelligence can achieve. Here, we delve into the detailed technical specifications that make Chat QA 270B a standout in the realm of AI.

At the core of Chat QA 270B is its unparalleled token capacity. With the ability to handle 128,000 tokens, this model can process vast amounts of text—equivalent to about 100 pages—in a single instance. This immense capacity is crucial for tasks requiring deep understanding and extensive context, allowing the model to maintain coherence and relevance over long passages of information.

The architecture of Chat QA 270B is built on a sophisticated neural network design, optimized for both performance and scalability. This design leverages Nvidia's state-of-the-art hardware, including the latest GPUs, to deliver high-speed processing and efficient resource utilization. The integration of these advanced hardware components ensures that the model operates smoothly even under demanding conditions, handling large datasets and complex computations with ease.

One of the standout features of Chat QA 270B is its adaptability to different context lengths. While its primary strength lies in long-form content processing, it is equally adept at managing medium-length (32,000 tokens) and short-context (4,000 tokens) tasks. This versatility is achieved through a dynamic context management system, which adjusts the model's processing approach based on the length and complexity of the input. This system ensures optimal performance across a variety of applications, from generating detailed reports to answering concise queries.

The model's pre-training phase involved a diverse dataset that emphasized long sequences, providing a rich foundation for its extended context capabilities. This dataset, known as Slim Pajama, encompasses a wide range of topics and formats, enabling Chat QA 270B to develop a comprehensive understanding of language patterns and structures. The pre-training was conducted using advanced algorithms that optimize the model's ability to process and generate text, ensuring high accuracy and relevance.

Following the pre-training, Chat QA 270B underwent a three-stage instruction tuning process. This process involved fine-tuning the model's responses to align with real-world applications, enhancing its ability to apply knowledge effectively. The instruction tuning stages were designed to mimic human learning, focusing on creativity, problem-solving, and contextual understanding.

This approach has equipped Chat QA 270B with the capability to handle complex, nuanced tasks that require more than just rote memorization.

An integral part of Chat QA 270B's technical prowess is its implementation of Retrieval-Augmented Generation (RAG). RAG allows the model to break down extensive tasks into manageable chunks, retrieving relevant information as needed. This method not only enhances the model's efficiency but also improves the accuracy and relevance of its outputs. By mimicking human problem-solving strategies, RAG enables Chat QA 270B to tackle tasks that require deep, contextual insights and adaptive reasoning.

In terms of performance benchmarks, Chat QA 270B has demonstrated exceptional results. In long-context tasks, it significantly outperforms many of its competitors, showcasing its superior capability in handling extensive information. Even in medium-length and short-context scenarios, the model maintains high performance, consistently delivering accurate and coherent outputs. These benchmarks highlight the robustness and versatility of Chat QA 270B, reinforcing its position as a leading AI model.

Overall, the technical specifications of Nvidia's Chat QA 270B reflect a model that is at the cutting edge of AI technology. Its vast token capacity, advanced neural network architecture, dynamic context management, comprehensive pre-training, and innovative RAG implementation collectively contribute to its outstanding performance. As a result, Chat QA 270B stands ready to revolutionize various industries, offering unprecedented capabilities in information processing and generation.

The performance benchmarks of Nvidia's Chat QA 270B are a testament to its advanced capabilities and robust design. This AI model has been meticulously tested across various scenarios, including long context tasks, medium-length tasks, and short context scenarios. These benchmarks highlight its superiority in handling diverse and complex challenges, establishing it as a leader in the field.

In long context tasks, Chat QA 270B truly shines. Its ability to process 128,000 tokens allows it to manage extensive passages of text with remarkable coherence and accuracy. This capability is particularly beneficial for applications that require a deep understanding of long documents, such as academic research, legal analysis, and content creation. In benchmark tests, Chat QA 270B has consistently outperformed other models, including GPT-4 Turbo. For instance, on infinite bench long context tasks, it achieved a score of 34.116086076 T4 Turbos, demonstrating its exceptional proficiency in handling large volumes of information.

When it comes to medium-length tasks, Chat QA 270B continues to exhibit impressive performance. These tasks, which typically involve around 32,000 tokens, require a balance between depth and brevity. Chat QA 270B's dynamic context management system ensures that it can seamlessly transition between processing long and medium-length inputs without compromising on accuracy or relevance. Although it slightly trails behind GPT-4 Turbo in some medium-length tasks, it still holds a competitive edge over many other models, showcasing its versatility and adaptability.

In short context scenarios, which involve around 4,000 tokens, Chat QA 270B proves its capability to manage concise and direct queries effectively. It scored 54.81 in short-context benchmarks, surpassing both GPT-4 Turbo and Quen 272 B Instruct. This makes it a valuable tool for applications such as customer service, quick information retrieval, and real-time assistance, where prompt and precise responses are crucial.

One of the unique features of Chat QA 270B is its sophisticated pre-training on long sequences. This foundational step involved training the model on a mix of data, known as Slim Pajama, which emphasizes long sequences of text. This approach laid the groundwork for the model's extended context abilities, ensuring it can handle complex and lengthy inputs with ease. The pre-training phase was designed to optimize the model's understanding of language patterns and structures, equipping it with a robust foundation for subsequent tuning and application.

The three-stage instruction tuning process further distinguishes Chat QA 270B from other models. This process involves fine-tuning the model's responses to align with real-world applications, enhancing its ability to apply knowledge creatively and effectively. The three stages of instruction tuning mimic human learning processes, focusing on creativity, problem-solving, and contextual understanding. This method has significantly improved the model's performance across various tasks, making it a versatile and reliable tool for diverse applications.

Chat QA 270B's implementation of Retrieval-Augmented Generation (RAG) is another groundbreaking innovation. RAG allows the model to break down large tasks into manageable chunks and retrieve relevant information as needed. This approach mimics human problem-solving strategies, enhancing the model's efficiency and accuracy in handling extensive and complex tasks. RAG's effectiveness is particularly evident in scenarios requiring deep contextual insights and adaptive reasoning, making Chat QA 270B a formidable tool in fields such as scientific research, legal analysis, and content creation.

In summary, the performance benchmarks and unique features of Nvidia's Chat QA 270B underscore its advanced capabilities and innovative design. Its exceptional performance in long context tasks, competitive edge in medium-length tasks, and impressive handling of short context scenarios highlight its versatility and robustness. The combination of sophisticated pre-training, the three-stage instruction tuning process, and the innovative RAG implementation positions Chat QA 270B as a leading AI model, ready to revolutionize various industries and applications. As we continue to explore its capabilities and applications, the true potential of this technological marvel becomes increasingly apparent, promising to reshape the future of AI.

Chapter 3: The Power of Retrieval-Augmented Generation (RAG)

Nvidia's Chat QA 270B introduces a sophisticated technique known as Retrieval-Augmented Generation, or RAG, which significantly enhances its ability to process and generate text. This innovative approach sets Chat QA 270B apart from other AI models, allowing it to tackle tasks that require a deep understanding of vast amounts of information.

Retrieval-Augmented Generation operates on a principle similar to how humans approach complex problems. When faced with a large task, we often break it down into smaller, more manageable parts and retrieve relevant information as needed to piece together a coherent response. RAG leverages this strategy to improve the efficiency and effectiveness of AI in handling extensive context.

At its core, RAG works by integrating two key components: a retriever and a generator. The retriever is responsible for sifting through a vast repository of data to find the most relevant pieces of information related to the task at hand. This step ensures that the AI has access to the most pertinent data, much like how a researcher might gather reference materials before writing a paper.

Once the relevant information is retrieved, the generator takes over. This component synthesizes the retrieved data, combining it with the model's pre-existing knowledge to produce a comprehensive and coherent response. The generator ensures that the output is contextually relevant and logically structured, making it suitable for a wide range of applications, from answering complex queries to generating detailed reports.

One of the significant advantages of RAG is its ability to handle extremely long contexts efficiently. Traditional AI models often struggle with maintaining coherence and relevance when processing large volumes of text. RAG mitigates this challenge by dynamically retrieving and incorporating information as needed, ensuring that the model can generate accurate and contextually appropriate responses regardless of the input length.

The implementation of RAG in Chat QA 270B is particularly effective for tasks beyond 100,000 tokens, where brute force methods fall short. By breaking down extensive tasks into manageable chunks, RAG enables the model to approach problems in a more nuanced and sophisticated manner. This approach not only improves the accuracy and relevance of the generated responses but also enhances the model's overall efficiency.

Moreover, RAG's retrieval-based strategy mimics human cognitive processes, making Chat QA 270B more adept at handling real-world tasks. This capability is especially beneficial in scenarios that require deep contextual understanding and adaptive reasoning, such as legal analysis, scientific research, and long-form content creation.

In essence, RAG represents a significant advancement in AI technology, enhancing the capabilities of models like Chat QA 270B. By integrating retrieval and generation processes, RAG enables the model to handle extensive and complex tasks with remarkable efficiency and accuracy. This innovation is a testament to Nvidia's commitment to pushing the boundaries of what AI can achieve, offering a glimpse into the future of intelligent information processing.

The benefits of Retrieval-Augmented Generation (RAG) in long context processing are profound, positioning Nvidia's Chat QA 270B as a transformative tool in the AI landscape. RAG's approach addresses the limitations faced by traditional AI models, enabling more sophisticated and accurate handling of extensive information.

One of the primary benefits of RAG in long context processing is its ability to maintain coherence and relevance across large volumes of text. Traditional AI models often struggle with lengthy inputs, as they can lose track of the context, leading to fragmented or inaccurate responses. RAG overcomes this by dynamically retrieving the most pertinent information, ensuring that the model remains focused on the relevant aspects of the input throughout the processing. This results in outputs that are not only more coherent but also contextually appropriate, even when dealing with extensive text.

Another significant advantage of RAG is its efficiency in managing large datasets. In traditional models, processing long contexts requires vast computational resources and can be time-consuming. RAG, however, streamlines this process by breaking down the task into smaller, more manageable parts. This division allows the model to handle each segment effectively, reducing the overall computational load and improving processing speed. Consequently, RAG-equipped models like Chat QA 270B can deliver faster and more efficient performance, making them suitable for real-time applications and tasks requiring quick turnaround times.

RAG's retrieval-based approach also enhances the model's accuracy. By accessing a vast repository of data and retrieving only the most relevant pieces, RAG ensures that the generated responses are grounded in accurate and up-to-date information. This capability is crucial for tasks that demand high precision, such as legal analysis, scientific research, and detailed report generation. Traditional models, which often rely on pre-existing knowledge without dynamic retrieval, can fall short in these scenarios, as they may not incorporate the most current or relevant data.

Moreover, RAG's ability to handle long contexts with nuanced understanding sets it apart from traditional models. Traditional AI models are generally designed to operate within fixed context windows, making them less adaptable to varying input lengths. In contrast, RAG's dynamic retrieval system allows it to adjust to different context lengths seamlessly. Whether the input is a short query or an extensive document, RAG can efficiently manage the information, providing accurate and coherent outputs regardless of the context size.

When comparing RAG to traditional AI models, the differences in their approach and capabilities become evident. Traditional models typically rely on a single, continuous processing of the input data, which can lead to issues with coherence and context retention, especially for long texts. These models may also struggle with integrating new information dynamically, limiting their ability to provide the most relevant and accurate responses.

In contrast, RAG-equipped models like Chat QA 270B adopt a more sophisticated approach by incorporating retrieval and generation processes. This dual mechanism allows RAG to access and utilize vast amounts of data dynamically, ensuring that the model remains informed and accurate. The retrieval component actively searches for relevant information, while the generation component synthesizes this data with the model's pre-existing knowledge, resulting in outputs that are both contextually rich and accurate.

Furthermore, traditional models often require extensive computational resources to process long contexts, making them less efficient and more costly to operate. RAG's method of breaking down tasks into smaller segments not only improves processing efficiency but also reduces the computational burden. This makes RAG-equipped models more scalable and practical for a wide range of applications, from real-time customer service to in-depth research analysis.

In summary, the benefits of RAG in long context processing are manifold, enhancing the capabilities of AI models like Nvidia's Chat QA 270B. By maintaining coherence, improving efficiency, and ensuring accuracy, RAG addresses the limitations of traditional AI models, offering a more sophisticated and effective solution for handling extensive and complex information. This innovation underscores the transformative potential of RAG in advancing AI technology and its applications across various fields.

Chapter 4: Diverse Applications of Llama 3 Chat QA 270B

Nvidia's Chat QA 270B opens up a world of possibilities with its diverse applications, transforming how we approach tasks across various fields. Its advanced capabilities make it an invaluable tool in content creation, the legal profession, scientific research, customer service, education, business decision-making, and marketing and advertising. Each application showcases the model's ability to handle complex tasks with remarkable efficiency and accuracy, redefining what is possible with AI.

In the realm of content creation, Chat QA 270B excels at writing long-form articles and books. Its ability to process 128,000 tokens ensures that it can manage extensive narratives without losing coherence or relevance. This makes it an ideal companion for authors and journalists who need to generate detailed, in-depth content. Whether it's crafting a novel, composing an in-depth investigative report, or writing a comprehensive academic paper, Chat QA 270B maintains a consistent narrative flow, ensuring that the final output is engaging and well-structured.

The legal profession benefits significantly from Chat QA 270B's capabilities. Document review and case research, traditionally time-consuming tasks, become streamlined with the model's advanced text processing abilities. Legal professionals can leverage Chat QA 270B to analyze entire legal libraries in seconds, identifying relevant precedents and key pieces of information that would otherwise take hours to find. This not only accelerates the research process but also enhances the accuracy and thoroughness of legal analysis, leading to better-informed decisions and strategies.

In scientific research, Chat QA 270B proves to be an invaluable asset. Researchers can use the model to sift through vast amounts of literature, quickly identifying patterns and connections that might elude human analysis. This capability accelerates the pace of discovery across various fields, from medicine to environmental science. By providing detailed summaries and insights, Chat QA 270B helps researchers stay up-to-date with the latest developments and focus on the most promising avenues for further investigation.

Customer service is another area where Chat QA 270B's impact is profound. The model's ability to enhance chatbots and virtual assistants leads to more sophisticated and responsive customer interactions. It can handle complex multi-part queries, providing users with accurate and contextually appropriate responses. This not only improves the customer experience but also reduces the workload on human representatives, allowing them to focus on more intricate issues that require a personal touch.

In education, Chat QA 270B powers personalized learning systems that adapt to each student's needs and learning style. The model can generate custom study materials, provide detailed explanations, and even simulate one-on-one tutoring sessions. This personalized approach helps students grasp difficult concepts more effectively and progress at their own pace, making learning more engaging and effective.

Business decision-making is greatly enhanced by Chat QA 270B's ability to analyze vast amounts of market data, financial reports, and industry trends. The model provides crucial insights for strategic planning and risk assessment, helping businesses make informed decisions. By identifying patterns and predicting market movements, Chat QA 270B aids in developing strategies that are both proactive and responsive to the dynamic business environment.

In the field of marketing and advertising, Chat QA 270B's ability to generate nuanced, context-appropriate content is a game-changer. Marketers can use the model to create personalized campaigns that resonate with target audiences. Whether it's crafting compelling ad copy, developing engaging social media posts, or generating detailed customer insights, Chat QA 270B ensures that the content is both relevant and impactful, leading to more effective marketing efforts.

The diverse applications of Nvidia's Chat QA 270B demonstrate its transformative potential across various fields. Its advanced capabilities in content creation, legal analysis, scientific research, customer service, education, business decision-making, and marketing highlight the model's versatility and efficiency. As AI continues to evolve, Chat QA 270B stands as a testament to the remarkable possibilities that advanced technology can bring, driving innovation and enhancing productivity in countless ways.

Chapter 5: Performance Highlights and Limitations

Nvidia's Chat QA 270B excels in a variety of tasks, showcasing particular strengths in handling long context tasks while also facing challenges in medium-length tasks. Understanding these strengths and challenges, along with areas for improvement and insights from benchmark tests, provides a comprehensive view of the model's capabilities and potential.

One of the primary strengths of Chat QA 270B lies in its ability to manage long context tasks. With a token capacity of 128,000, the model can process extensive amounts of text, equivalent to about 100 pages, without losing coherence or accuracy. This makes it particularly effective for applications requiring deep contextual understanding, such as writing detailed reports, analyzing lengthy legal documents, or conducting comprehensive literature reviews. The model's ability to maintain a consistent narrative flow over long passages is a significant advantage, ensuring that the output remains relevant and logically structured.

However, Chat QA 270B does face some challenges when it comes to medium-length tasks. These tasks, typically involving around 32,000 tokens, require a delicate balance between depth and brevity. While the model is highly capable, it occasionally struggles to maintain the same level of coherence and relevance in these mid-range tasks as it does in longer or shorter contexts. This indicates an area where further refinement could enhance its performance, ensuring that it can handle medium-length inputs with the same efficiency and accuracy as it does with longer texts.

There are several areas for improvement that could elevate Chat QA 270B's performance even further. One such area is enhancing its nuanced understanding and reasoning capabilities, particularly in medium-length tasks. Improving the model's ability to transition seamlessly between different context lengths without compromising on the quality of the output would make it even more versatile. Additionally, optimizing the model's computational efficiency could help reduce resource consumption and processing times, making it more accessible and practical for a wider range of applications.

Insights from benchmark tests provide valuable data on Chat QA 270B's performance across various scenarios. In long context tasks, the model has consistently outperformed its competitors, demonstrating its superior ability to handle extensive information. For instance, it achieved a score of 34.116086076 T4 Turbos in long-context benchmarks, showcasing its exceptional proficiency. In medium-length tasks, while still competitive, the model shows some variability in performance, indicating room for optimization. Short context scenarios, involving around 4,000 tokens, also highlight the model's strength, with a score of 54.81, surpassing both GPT-4 Turbo and Quen 272 B Instruct.

These benchmark results underscore Chat QA 270B's robust capabilities and potential for further development. The model's strengths in long context tasks position it as an invaluable tool for applications requiring detailed and coherent analysis of extensive texts. Addressing the challenges in medium-length tasks and optimizing performance across different context lengths will enhance its versatility, making it even more effective for a broader range of uses.

In summary, Nvidia's Chat QA 270B stands out for its impressive performance in long context tasks, providing coherent and relevant outputs even with extensive texts. While it faces challenges in medium-length tasks, ongoing improvements and optimizations hold the promise of overcoming these hurdles. Insights from benchmark tests highlight the model's strengths and areas for growth, paving the way for continued advancements in AI technology. As we refine and enhance models like Chat QA 270B, the future of AI-driven solutions looks increasingly promising, offering unprecedented capabilities across diverse fields and applications.

Chapter 6: Environmental and Ethical Considerations

As powerful as Nvidia's Chat QA 270B is, its deployment and operation come with significant considerations regarding energy consumption, environmental impact, ethical implications, potential misuse, bias, misinformation, and privacy concerns. Addressing these issues is crucial to ensure that the benefits of this advanced AI model are maximized while minimizing potential risks and drawbacks.

One of the primary concerns with large AI models like Chat QA 270B is energy consumption and the subsequent environmental impact. Training and running such extensive models require substantial computational resources, which translates into high energy usage. The energy required to maintain and operate these systems can be considerable, contributing to a larger carbon footprint. As AI technology continues to advance, it becomes imperative to develop more energy-efficient algorithms and leverage sustainable energy sources to mitigate the environmental impact.

Ethical implications are another significant consideration when it comes to deploying advanced AI models. The capabilities of Chat QA 270B raise questions about the responsible use of AI technology. Ensuring that the model is used ethically involves addressing issues such as bias, fairness, and the potential for misuse. AI models are trained on vast datasets that may contain inherent biases, which can be perpetuated or even amplified by the model. It is essential to implement robust mechanisms to detect, mitigate, and correct biases in the training data and model outputs to ensure fairness and equity.

Potential misuse of AI models is a critical concern that needs careful attention. The advanced capabilities of Chat QA 270B can be exploited for malicious purposes, such as generating convincing misinformation, deepfakes, or other forms of deceptive content. This misuse can have far-reaching consequences, from undermining public trust to impacting democratic processes and social stability. Developing and enforcing ethical guidelines and regulations, along with creating technologies to detect and prevent misuse, is essential to safeguard against these risks.

Issues of bias and misinformation are particularly challenging. AI models trained on large datasets can inadvertently learn and propagate biases present in the data. This can lead to biased outputs that reinforce stereotypes or marginalize certain groups. Moreover, the ability to generate realistic and persuasive content increases the risk of spreading misinformation. Addressing these issues requires a multifaceted approach, including improving the diversity and representativeness of training data, implementing bias detection and mitigation techniques, and promoting digital literacy to help users critically evaluate AI-generated content.

Privacy concerns are paramount in the context of AI. The ability of models like Chat QA 270B to process and generate vast amounts of text raises questions about data security and individual privacy. Ensuring that sensitive information is protected and that AI systems comply with privacy regulations is critical. Developing robust anonymization techniques and secure data handling practices can help mitigate privacy risks. Additionally, creating transparent AI systems that allow users to understand how their data is used and ensuring informed consent are essential steps toward protecting privacy.

As we continue to integrate AI models like Chat QA 270B into various applications, it is vital to balance innovation with responsibility. Addressing energy consumption and environmental impact involves adopting sustainable practices and advancing energy-efficient technologies. Ethical implications, potential misuse, issues of bias and misinformation, and privacy concerns require continuous vigilance, proactive measures, and collaboration among technologists, policymakers, and ethicists.

Ultimately, the goal is to harness the power of AI in ways that benefit society while minimizing risks. By prioritizing ethical considerations, promoting transparency, and ensuring fairness, we can pave the way for a future where AI enhances human capabilities and drives positive change. Nvidia's Chat QA 270B represents a significant step forward in AI technology, and with thoughtful and responsible deployment, it has the potential to contribute meaningfully to various fields while addressing the critical challenges it presents.

Chapter 7: Future Prospects and Societal Impact

The future advancements in AI promise to be as exciting as they are transformative, with Nvidia's Chat QA 270B leading the charge in redefining the possibilities of artificial intelligence. As we look ahead, several key trends and dynamics are poised to shape the AI landscape, including the competition between open-source and proprietary models, the impacts on various fields such as healthcare and education, and the profound philosophical and geopolitical questions that accompany these technological breakthroughs.

The rapid pace of AI development suggests that future advancements will continue to push the boundaries of what is possible. We can expect models to become even more sophisticated, with enhanced capabilities for understanding and generating human-like text. Improvements in context handling, reasoning, and adaptability will make AI models more versatile and applicable across an even broader range of tasks. Innovations in machine learning algorithms and hardware acceleration will further drive the efficiency and performance of AI, making advanced models more accessible and cost-effective.

One of the significant dynamics shaping the future of AI is the competition between open-source and proprietary models. Open-source models, like those based on Meta's Llama 3 framework, foster collaboration and innovation by making cutting-edge technology accessible to a wide audience. They allow researchers and developers to build on existing work, accelerating the pace of advancements. On the other hand, proprietary models, developed by companies like Nvidia and OpenAI, often come with significant resources and funding that can drive high-quality, robust solutions tailored for specific applications. This competition is likely to intensify, leading to rapid advancements and a diverse ecosystem of AI technologies that benefit users and developers alike.

The impacts of AI on various fields are profound. In healthcare, AI models like Chat QA 270B can revolutionize diagnostics and treatment by analyzing large volumes of medical data to identify patterns and anomalies that might be missed by human eyes. This capability can lead to more accurate diagnoses, personalized treatment plans, and a deeper understanding of diseases. Additionally, AI can streamline administrative tasks, reduce healthcare costs, and improve patient outcomes by enabling faster and more efficient processes.

The job market and education systems will also experience significant shifts due to AI advancements. While some roles may become obsolete, new opportunities will emerge, requiring a reimagining of workforce training and education. AI will augment human capabilities, leading to the creation of new jobs that focus on managing, collaborating with, and leveraging AI technologies. Education systems will need to evolve to equip future generations with the skills necessary to thrive in an AI-driven world, emphasizing critical thinking, creativity, and ethical reasoning.

Philosophical questions about creativity and consciousness will become increasingly relevant as AI models like Chat QA 270B continue to advance. Can a machine truly create something original, or is it limited to recombining existing information in novel ways? These questions challenge our understanding of creativity and the nature of consciousness, prompting deep reflections on what it means to be human. As AI becomes more capable, these philosophical debates will gain prominence, influencing how we perceive and integrate AI into our lives.

Geopolitical implications and AI governance are critical considerations as AI technology continues to evolve. The development of advanced AI models has far-reaching implications for global power dynamics, with countries and regions vying for leadership in AI technology. This competition could lead to a new kind of technological arms race, raising questions about the governance and ethical use of AI on a global scale. Ensuring responsible and ethical use of AI across different cultures and political systems will require international collaboration and the establishment of robust governance frameworks.

AI governance involves addressing issues such as data privacy, security, bias, and transparency. Developing standards and regulations that promote ethical AI practices while fostering innovation is essential. International cooperation will be crucial in creating a balanced approach that maximizes the benefits of AI while mitigating its risks.

In conclusion, the future of AI, exemplified by models like Nvidia's Chat QA 270B, is poised to bring transformative changes across various fields and aspects of life. As we navigate this new era, it is essential to balance innovation with ethical considerations, ensuring that AI technologies are developed and deployed responsibly. By addressing the challenges and opportunities presented by AI, we can harness its potential to drive positive change, enhance human capabilities, and contribute to solving some of the most pressing issues of our time.

Chapter 8: Navigating Ethical AI Development

Addressing bias and ensuring fairness in AI models like Nvidia's Chat QA 270B is critical for building systems that are trustworthy and equitable. Bias in AI can arise from various sources, including the data used for training, the design of the algorithms, and the deployment context. Addressing these biases requires a multi-faceted approach that includes improving the diversity of training data, implementing robust bias detection and mitigation techniques, and fostering a culture of fairness and accountability in AI development.

One of the first steps in addressing bias is to ensure that the training data is diverse and representative of different populations and scenarios. This helps prevent the model from learning and perpetuating biases present in the data. Additionally, developing algorithms that can detect and correct biases during the training process is essential. These algorithms can identify biased patterns and adjust the model's learning process to promote fairness. Regular audits and evaluations of AI models can also help ensure that they continue to perform fairly over time and across different applications.

Transparency and explainability are crucial for building trust in AI systems. Users and stakeholders need to understand how AI models like Chat QA 270B make decisions and generate outputs. This involves creating models that can explain their reasoning and provide insights into their decision-making processes. Techniques such as model interpretability, where the internal workings of the model are made understandable to humans, and explainable AI (XAI), which focuses on creating AI systems that can explain their actions, are essential for achieving transparency. Providing clear documentation and user guides can also help users understand the capabilities and limitations of the AI models.

High-stakes applications, such as healthcare diagnostics and financial risk assessment, require particular attention to bias, fairness, transparency, and explainability. In healthcare diagnostics, AI models can assist doctors in identifying diseases, predicting patient outcomes, and personalizing treatment plans. However, biases in the model can lead to disparities in healthcare outcomes, disproportionately affecting certain populations. Ensuring fairness in healthcare AI involves rigorous testing, validation, and continuous monitoring to detect and mitigate biases. Transparency in how the AI reaches its conclusions is also vital for doctors to trust and effectively use the AI's recommendations.

Financial risk assessment is another area where AI can have significant impacts. AI models can analyze vast amounts of financial data to predict risks, assess creditworthiness, and detect fraudulent activities. However, biases in these models can result in unfair lending practices and financial exclusion. Ensuring fairness in financial AI involves using unbiased data, implementing fair lending algorithms, and providing transparency in the decision-making process. This helps build trust with consumers and regulatory bodies and ensures that AI contributes to equitable financial practices.

Combating misinformation and deepfakes is an increasingly important application of AI. The ability to generate realistic but false information poses a significant threat to public trust and social stability. AI models like Chat QA 270B can be used to detect and counteract misinformation by analyzing content for accuracy, identifying deepfakes, and providing verified information. Developing AI systems that can distinguish between true and false information requires advanced algorithms and continuous updates to keep up with the evolving tactics of misinformation creators. Transparency in how these systems operate and make decisions is also crucial for public trust.

In summary, addressing bias and ensuring fairness in AI involves diverse training data, robust bias detection and mitigation techniques, and a commitment to accountability. Transparency and explainability are essential for building trust and understanding in AI systems. High-stakes applications like healthcare diagnostics and financial risk assessment require rigorous testing and monitoring to ensure fair and transparent outcomes. Combating misinformation and deepfakes involves advanced detection algorithms and clear communication about how these systems work. By prioritizing these principles, we can develop AI systems that are not only powerful but also ethical and trustworthy, contributing positively to society.

Chapter 9: Collaborative AI Systems

The potential for collaborative AI systems represents a significant advancement in the field of artificial intelligence. As AI models like Nvidia's Chat QA 270B continue to evolve, the idea of integrating multiple specialized AI systems to work together becomes increasingly feasible and advantageous. Collaborative AI systems can leverage the strengths of various models to tackle complex problems more effectively, driving innovation and discovery in scientific research and other fields.

Collaborative AI systems involve the integration of multiple AI models, each specialized in different tasks or domains, to work together harmoniously. This approach allows for the combination of diverse capabilities, leading to more comprehensive and robust solutions. For instance, one model might excel at natural language processing, while another specializes in image recognition or data analysis. By working together, these models can provide a multifaceted approach to problem-solving, offering insights and solutions that a single model could not achieve on its own.

In scientific research, the potential applications of collaborative AI systems are vast and transformative. Research often involves analyzing complex datasets, identifying patterns, and generating hypotheses that require interdisciplinary knowledge. Collaborative AI systems can bring together models trained in different scientific domains, enabling researchers to conduct more thorough and efficient analyses. For example, a collaborative AI system could integrate a model specialized in genomics with another focused on environmental data to study the impacts of climate change on genetic diversity.

One of the primary benefits of collaborative AI systems in scientific research is their ability to process and synthesize large volumes of data from various sources. This capability is particularly valuable in fields such as medicine, where researchers need to analyze genetic data, clinical trials, patient records, and environmental factors to understand diseases and develop treatments. Collaborative AI systems can provide a holistic view of the data, uncovering correlations and insights that might be missed by individual models. This can accelerate the pace of discovery and lead to more effective and personalized healthcare solutions.

Collaborative AI systems also excel in problem-solving by breaking down complex issues into manageable components and addressing each part with specialized expertise. For instance, in the field of drug discovery, a collaborative AI system might combine models that predict chemical properties, simulate biological interactions, and analyze clinical trial data. This integrated approach can streamline the drug development process, reducing costs and time while increasing the likelihood of identifying promising candidates.

Moreover, collaborative AI systems can enhance the accuracy and reliability of research findings. By cross-referencing results from different models, researchers can validate their hypotheses and ensure that conclusions are based on robust and diverse data sources. This multidisciplinary approach reduces the risk of bias and error, leading to more credible and impactful scientific outcomes.

In addition to scientific research, collaborative AI systems have significant potential in other fields, such as engineering, economics, and social sciences. In engineering, for example, collaborative AI can integrate models that simulate physical systems, optimize designs, and predict performance under various conditions. This can lead to the development of more efficient and innovative technologies. In economics, collaborative AI systems can analyze market trends, model economic scenarios, and provide insights for policy-making and business strategy.

The development of collaborative AI systems also raises important considerations for AI governance and ethical use. Ensuring that these systems operate transparently and fairly is crucial for building trust and maximizing their benefits. Collaboration between technologists, ethicists, and policymakers will be essential to establish guidelines and standards that promote responsible AI development and deployment.

In summary, the potential for collaborative AI systems represents a significant leap forward in the capabilities of artificial intelligence. By integrating specialized AI models to work together, these systems can tackle complex problems more effectively, driving innovation and discovery across various fields. In scientific research, collaborative AI systems can process and synthesize large volumes of data, enhance accuracy, and accelerate the pace of discovery. The multidisciplinary approach of collaborative AI systems promises to transform not only science but also engineering, economics, and beyond, paving the way for a future where AI enhances human capabilities and drives progress in unprecedented ways.

Chapter 10: Privacy and Data Security

Balancing the benefits of AI with the need for privacy protection is one of the most critical challenges in the development and deployment of advanced AI systems like Nvidia's Chat QA 270B. As AI becomes more integrated into various aspects of our lives, ensuring that sensitive data is protected and user privacy is maintained is essential. Achieving this balance requires robust anonymization techniques and a reimagined approach to data ownership and consent.

One of the primary methods for protecting privacy in AI systems is through robust anonymization techniques. Anonymization involves removing or altering personal identifiers within datasets so that individuals cannot be readily identified. This process is crucial for ensuring that sensitive information remains confidential and that users' privacy is safeguarded. Advanced anonymization techniques include data masking, where specific data elements are obscured; generalization, where data is replaced with more generic values; and data perturbation, where data is slightly modified to protect individual identities while preserving overall data utility.

Implementing these techniques effectively requires a careful balance. The anonymization process must sufficiently protect individual privacy while maintaining the data's usefulness for AI training and analysis. Over-anonymization can lead to loss of valuable information, reducing the effectiveness of the AI model. Conversely, under-anonymization can leave individuals' data vulnerable to re-identification. Therefore, developing and employing sophisticated anonymization algorithms that strike this balance is crucial.

Reimagining data ownership and consent is another vital aspect of ensuring privacy protection in the age of AI. Traditional models of data ownership often place control in the hands of organizations that collect and process the data, rather than the individuals to whom the data pertains. This approach can lead to privacy concerns, as individuals may have limited visibility and control over how their data is used. Reimagining data ownership involves shifting the paradigm to empower individuals with greater control and rights over their data.

One approach to reimagining data ownership is through the concept of data sovereignty, where individuals retain ownership of their data and have the right to control its usage. This can be facilitated by technologies such as blockchain, which can provide transparent and secure mechanisms for managing data access and consent. Blockchain can enable individuals to grant and revoke access to their data dynamically, ensuring that they remain in control of their personal information at all times.

Consent management is also a critical component of reimagined data ownership. Informed consent processes must be designed to ensure that individuals fully understand how their data will be used and the implications of sharing their information. Consent should be granular, allowing individuals to specify which types of data can be used and for what purposes. Additionally, consent should be dynamic, enabling users to update their preferences and withdraw consent as needed. Implementing user-friendly interfaces and clear communication strategies is essential for achieving effective consent management.

Balancing AI benefits with privacy protection also involves adopting privacy-by-design principles in the development of AI systems. This approach integrates privacy considerations into every stage of the AI development lifecycle, from initial design to deployment and beyond. Privacy-by-design ensures that data protection measures are not just an afterthought but are embedded into the core architecture of AI systems. This includes implementing strong encryption, secure data storage, and rigorous access controls to prevent unauthorized data access.

Moreover, regulatory frameworks play a crucial role in protecting privacy in the context of AI. Regulations such as the General Data Protection Regulation (GDPR) in Europe set stringent standards for data protection and privacy, mandating organizations to adopt robust measures for data security and user consent. Compliance with such regulations ensures that AI systems operate within legal and ethical boundaries, safeguarding users' rights and privacy.

In conclusion, balancing the benefits of AI with privacy protection requires a multi-faceted approach that includes robust anonymization techniques, reimagined data ownership and consent models, privacy-by-design principles, and regulatory compliance. By implementing these strategies, we can harness the transformative potential of AI while ensuring that individuals' privacy is respected and protected. This balance is essential for building trust in AI systems and enabling their widespread adoption in a manner that benefits society as a whole.

Chapter 11: The Road Ahead

The development and deployment of advanced AI systems like Nvidia's Chat QA 270B necessitate a collaborative approach that transcends traditional disciplinary boundaries. Interdisciplinary collaboration brings together experts from various fields to address the complex challenges and opportunities presented by AI. This approach is essential for fostering innovation, ensuring ethical considerations are addressed, and maximizing the societal benefits of AI technologies.

Interdisciplinary collaboration in AI development involves the integration of knowledge and expertise from diverse fields such as computer science, ethics, law, psychology, sociology, and economics. By bringing together technologists with ethicists, policymakers, and domain experts, we can create AI systems that are not only technologically advanced but also ethically sound and socially responsible. For instance, ethicists can help identify potential biases and ethical dilemmas, while legal experts can ensure compliance with regulations and standards. Sociologists and psychologists can provide insights into the societal impacts of AI, helping to design systems that are more user-friendly and culturally sensitive.

Moreover, interdisciplinary collaboration can drive innovation by combining different perspectives and approaches. In the development of Chat QA 270B, collaboration between researchers specializing in natural language processing, machine learning, and data science led to the creation of a model that excels in understanding and generating human-like text. This collaborative effort ensures that the AI is robust, versatile, and capable of addressing a wide range of applications.

Education and workforce training are critical for preparing individuals to thrive in an AI-driven world. As AI continues to permeate various industries, the demand for skills in AI and related fields is growing rapidly. Education systems must adapt to equip students with the necessary knowledge and competencies to succeed in this new landscape. This includes not only technical skills such as programming, data analysis, and machine learning but also critical thinking, creativity, and ethical reasoning.

Integrating AI education into the curriculum at all levels, from primary schools to universities, can help build a foundation of knowledge and interest in AI. Hands-on learning experiences, such as coding projects, AI labs, and internships, can provide practical skills and real-world exposure. Additionally, interdisciplinary courses that combine AI with ethics, law, and social sciences can prepare students to navigate the complex implications of AI technologies.

Workforce training programs are equally important for current professionals who need to adapt to the changing job market. Continuous learning and upskilling initiatives can help workers acquire new skills and transition to roles that leverage AI technologies. Companies can play a significant role by offering training programs, workshops, and certifications in AI-related fields. Public-private partnerships can also facilitate broader access to training resources and support workforce development.

Shaping a future with AI enhancements requires a forward-thinking approach that prioritizes human-centric values and ethical considerations. AI has the potential to enhance human capabilities, drive scientific discovery, and solve global challenges, but this potential must be harnessed responsibly. By focusing on the following key areas, we can shape a future where AI benefits society as a whole:

1. **Ethical AI Development**: Ensuring that AI systems are developed and deployed ethically is paramount. This includes addressing issues such as bias, transparency, accountability, and fairness. Developing ethical guidelines and standards, and embedding ethical considerations into the AI development process, can help build trust and acceptance of AI technologies.
2. **Human-AI Collaboration**: Emphasizing the collaborative potential of AI and humans can lead to more effective and innovative solutions. AI should be seen as a tool that

augments human capabilities, rather than replacing them. Designing AI systems that enhance human decision-making, creativity, and problem-solving can lead to more productive and fulfilling outcomes.

3. **Inclusivity and Accessibility**: Ensuring that the benefits of AI are accessible to all individuals, regardless of socioeconomic status, geographic location, or other factors, is crucial. This involves making AI education and training widely available and designing AI systems that are inclusive and accessible to diverse populations.

4. **Sustainable AI**: Addressing the environmental impact of AI development and deployment is essential for long-term sustainability. This includes developing energy-efficient algorithms, using renewable energy sources, and minimizing the carbon footprint of AI systems.

5. **Global Cooperation**: Promoting international collaboration and cooperation in AI research, development, and governance can help address global challenges and ensure that AI benefits humanity as a whole. Establishing frameworks for responsible AI use across different cultures and political systems is essential for fostering a global AI ecosystem that is ethical and equitable.

In conclusion, interdisciplinary collaboration, education, and workforce training are fundamental for advancing AI development and preparing for an AI-driven future. By fostering collaboration across diverse fields, equipping individuals with the necessary skills, and prioritizing ethical and human-centric values, we can shape a future where AI enhances human potential and contributes positively to society.

Conclusion

As we reach the conclusion of our exploration of Nvidia's Chat QA 270B and the broader landscape of artificial intelligence, it's evident that we stand on the brink of a new era defined by remarkable technological advancements and profound societal impacts. This journey through the intricacies of AI development, applications, and ethical considerations has illuminated the vast potential and critical challenges that accompany these powerful tools.

Recapping the key points, we began with an introduction to Chat QA 270B, understanding its development by Nvidia and its foundation on Meta's Llama 3 framework. We delved into its impressive technical specifications, highlighting its 128,000 token capacity, versatile context handling, and sophisticated training processes. Performance benchmarks demonstrated its strengths in long context tasks, while also identifying areas for improvement in medium-length scenarios.

The narrative continued with an exploration of Retrieval-Augmented Generation (RAG), a pivotal feature that enhances the model's efficiency and accuracy by mimicking human problem-solving strategies. We examined the diverse applications of Chat QA 270B, from content creation and legal analysis to scientific research, customer service, education, business decision-making, and marketing. Each application showcased the model's transformative potential across various fields.

We addressed critical issues such as energy consumption, environmental impact, and ethical implications, emphasizing the importance of balancing AI benefits with privacy protection and ensuring transparency, fairness, and accountability. The discussion on future advancements in AI underscored the need for interdisciplinary collaboration, robust education, and workforce training to prepare for an AI-driven world.

Final thoughts on the future of AI highlight both the opportunities and responsibilities that lie ahead. AI models like Chat QA 270B have the potential to revolutionize industries, drive scientific discovery, and enhance human capabilities. However, realizing this potential requires a commitment to ethical development, transparency, and inclusivity. As AI becomes increasingly integrated into our lives, it is crucial to address issues of bias, misinformation, and privacy, ensuring that AI technologies are used responsibly and equitably.

As we look to the future, it is clear that the evolution of AI will continue to surprise, challenge, and inspire us. The rapid pace of advancements promises new breakthroughs, but also calls for thoughtful consideration of the ethical, social, and environmental implications. The journey ahead will require collaboration across disciplines, robust debate, and proactive measures to harness AI's power for the benefit of all.

In this spirit, a call to action for readers is essential. Whether you are a technologist, researcher, educator, policymaker, or simply a curious individual, your engagement with AI is vital. Embrace the opportunities for learning and innovation that AI presents. Advocate for ethical practices, transparency, and inclusivity in AI development. Participate in discussions and initiatives that shape the future of AI governance and policy. By taking an active role, you can contribute to a future where AI enhances human potential, drives positive change, and benefits society as a whole.

Thank you for joining this exploration of Nvidia's Chat QA 270B and the broader AI landscape. As we move forward, let us remain committed to fostering a world where technology and humanity thrive together, creating a better future for all.

www.ingramcontent.com/pod-product-compliance
Lightning Source LLC
Chambersburg PA
CBHW071951210526
45479CB00003B/898